LOW FAT
DREAM
DESSERTS

Consultant Editor:
Valerie Ferguson

HERMES
HOUSE

Contents

Introduction

If you're trying to cut down on fat in your diet, the chances are that the foods you most crave are the rich, sweet ones – lovely, luscious desserts and proper puddings. And the reason you crave them is that you think they're denied you when you're on a sensible low fat diet.

The good news is that you really do not have to give up puddings – if you stick to the recipes in this book. They're all specially designed to fit into a healthy, lighter diet and all have fewer than 5 g/⅛ oz fat per portion.

Nowadays, we're lucky enough to have available lots of delicious, wholesome alternatives to ingredients such as cream – so even classic, rich dishes can be lightened quite easily. You'll find that, after a while, your taste will change, and in many cases you will actually prefer the simpler, fresher flavours of low fat desserts to some of the over-rich alternatives.

We all know we should be eating more fruit – it's recommended that we should eat five pieces or portions of fresh fruit or vegetables each day, so it's important to include plenty of fresh fruit in your desserts for fibre, essential vitamins and minerals. These recipes make full use of the wonderfully abundant choice of fruits we now have all year round.

So whether you're reducing fat in order to lose weight, or just trying to lighten your diet, this book will help you do it without giving up the sweet things in life!

Planning a Low Fat Diet

Reducing the fat in your diet is not difficult if you follow the advice below.

The British Adult Survey reported that men eat, on average, 102 g/3½ oz fat a day and women 73.5 g/2½ oz. Yet just 10 g/¼ oz is all you really need as long as some of it is polyunsaturated to provide the 'essential' fatty acids. Fat is also necessary in the diet in order to provide the fat soluble vitamins, A, D, E and K.

Current nutritional advice is not quite that strict though and suggests that we should limit our daily fat intake to no more than 33% of total calories. In real terms, this means that for an average intake of 2,000 calories a day, 33% of energy would come from 660 calories or 73 g/2½ oz fat.

If you look at The Fat & Calorie Contents of Food chart, you will see how quickly you can consume this amount and how you can cut down. This is easy with obvious sources of fat, such as butter, cream, whole milk and cheeses, but watch out for 'hidden' fats in foods. For example, we tend to think of cakes as 'sweet' foods, but usually more calories come from their fat content. Fat makes up about half the weight of nuts. About 16% of the fat we eat comes from meat and meat products, 30% from cereal products such as biscuits, cakes and pastries, 13% from dairy products and eggs, 6% from fat spreads and 12% from vegetables including potatoes (which includes the oils/fats used to cook them).

There's now a great choice of dairy produce suitable for desserts; many of the products are low in fat, and make good substitutes for full fat ingredients such as cream.

BUTTER VS MARGARINE

Butter and margarine producers have spent a great deal on advertising, trying to convince us that their product is the healthiest. Both butter and margarine contain 82% fat and about the same number of calories (737 Kcals/3039 kJ in 100 g/3½ oz). Butter, however, is made up mainly of saturated fats (54%).

Fat is made up of three main types of fatty acids – saturated, mono-unsaturated and polyunsaturated. No food or oil is made up of just one type of fatty acid but is more likely to be a combination of all three. In health terms, it is the proportion of each that is important. The hardness or fluidity of a fat will give you some clue as to the type of fatty acids that make up a fat. Fats that are hard at room temperature such as butter and some margarines and cooking fats will contain a high proportion of saturated fats. Fats or oils high in mono-unsaturates such as olive oil tend to be 'mushy' or cloudy on a cold day while oils high in poly-unsaturates like sunflower or corn will

Make use of the natural sweetness and colour of the wide variety of fresh fruit in healthy puddings and desserts.

remain liquid even on a very cold day. Margarines high in polyunsaturates will always remain soft even when taken from the fridge.

Saturated fatty acids are believed to raise blood cholesterol levels and are thus considered to be unhealthy in excess; they are found mainly in foods of animal origin such as dairy foods (cream, full fat milk, cheese) and eggs. Mono-unsaturated fatty acids are generally considered healthy in moderation; the Mediterranean diet is relatively high in mono-unsaturated fatty acids – olive oil, olives, avocado pears. Polyunsaturated fatty acids are thought to promote a healthy blood circulation. They also provide 'essential fatty acids' which are essential components of all cell membranes. Polyunsaturates are found in vegetable and seed oils and margarines derived from them, oily fish and lean meat.

7

Low fat spreads or reduced fat butters contain 40% fat. There are also 'very low fat' spreads, containing 20–30% fat. They may not be suitable for cooking with and some are less palatable than others.

LABELLING
Look at labels when choosing food. Ingredients are always listed in order of quantity, so watch out for those with fat near the top as nutritional labels can be misleading.

Low fat
Contains less than half the fat of the standard product. Remember that some foods are very high in fat, so even if a product such as low fat spread has half the fat content of margarine it still contains quite a lot of fat (about 40 g per 100 g).

Reduced fat
Contains less than 75% of the fat of the standard product.

Low cholesterol
No more than 0.005% of the total fat is cholesterol.

High in polyunsaturates/low in saturates
Contains at least 35% fat of which at least 45% of the fatty acids are polyunsaturated and not more than 25% saturated.

The Fat & Calorie Contents of Food

The chart shows the weight of fat and the energy content of 25 g/1 oz of various foods.

FRUIT & NUTS	Fat	Energy
Apples	0.1 g	11 Kcal/45 kJ
Bananas	0.1 g	24 Kcal/101 kJ
Dried mixed fruit	0.1 g	67 Kcal/281 kJ
Grapefruit	0 g	8 Kcal/32 kJ
Oranges	0 g	9 Kcal/39 kJ
Peaches	0 g	8 Kcal/35 kJ
Almonds	14 g	153 Kcal/633 kJ
Brazil nuts	17 g	170 Kcal/703 kJ
Peanut butter, smooth	13.4 g	156 Kcal/645 kJ
Pine nuts	17.2 g	172 Kcal/710 kJ
Desiccated coconut	15.5 g	151 Kcal/623 kJ
Avocado	4.0 g	40 Kcal/190 kJ
Kiwi fruit	0.1 g	12 Kcal/52 kJ

OTHER FOODS	Fat	Energy
Sugar	0 g	98 Kcal/420 kJ
Chocolate, milk	7.6 g	132 Kcal/554 kJ
Honey	0 g	72 Kcal/301 kJ
Jam	0 g	65 Kcal/273 kJ
Marmalade	0 g	65 Kcal/273 kJ
Lemon curd	1.3 g	71 Kcal/301 kJ
Chocolate, plain	7.3 g	131 Kcal/549 kJ
Cocoa powder	5.4 g	78 Kcal/325 kJ

DAIRY PRODUCE, FATS & OILS	Fat	Energy
Cream, double	12 g	112 Kcal/462 kJ
Cream, single	4.8 g	49 Kcal/204 kJ
Cream, whipping	9.8 g	93 Kcal/385 kJ
Milk, skimmed	0 g	8 Kcal/35 kJ
Milk, whole	1 g	16 Kcal/69 kJ
Greek yogurt	2.3 g	29 Kcal/119 kJ
Low fat yogurt, natural	0.2 g	14 Kcal/59 kJ
Butter	20.4 g	184 Kcal/758 kJ
Low fat spread	10.1 g	97 Kcal/401 kJ
Margarine	20.4 g	185 Kcal/760 kJ
Corn oil	25 g	225 Kcal/924 kJ
Safflower oil	25 g	225 Kcal/924 kJ
Eggs (half an egg)	2.7 g	37 Kcal/153 kJ
Egg white	0 g	9 Kcal/38 kJ
Egg yolk	7.6 g	85 Kcal/351 kJ
Crème fraîche	10 g	95 Kcal/396 kJ
Crème fraîche, half fat	3.8 g	42 Kcal/173 kJ
Buttermilk	0.1 g	9 Kcal/39 kJ

Papaya Skewers with Passion Fruit Coulis

Tropical fruits, full of natural sweetness, make a simple exotic dessert.

Serves 6

INGREDIENTS
3 ripe papayas
10 passion fruit
    or kiwi fruit
30 ml/2 tbsp lime juice
30 ml/2 tbsp icing sugar
30 ml/2 tbsp white rum
toasted coconut and lime, to decorate

COOK'S TIP: If you are short of time, the passion fruit flesh can be used as it is, without puréeing or straining. Simply scoop the flesh from the skins and mix it with the fresh lime juice, sugar and rum. Kiwi fruit, however, will still need to be puréed.

2 Halve eight of the passion fruit or kiwi fruit and scoop out the flesh. Process the flesh for a few seconds in a blender or food processor.

3 Press the pulp through a strainer and discard the seeds. Add the lime juice, icing sugar and rum, and then stir well until the sugar has dissolved.

1 Cut the papayas in half and scoop out the seeds. Peel them and cut the flesh into even-size chunks. Thread the chunks on to six bamboo skewers.

Nutritional Notes	
Energy	94 Kcal/397 kJ
Fat, total	0.3 g
Saturated Fat	0.0 g
Cholesterol	0.0 mg

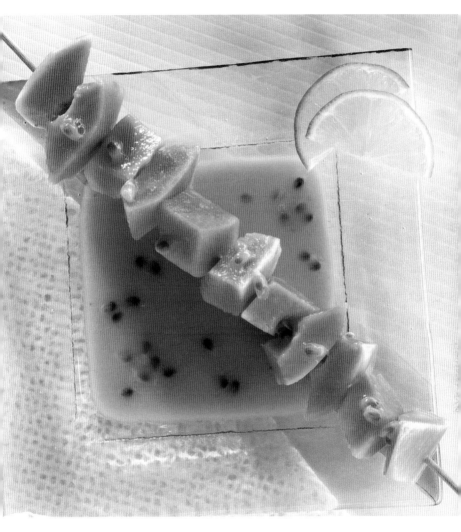

4 Spoon a little of the coulis on to six serving plates. Place the papaya skewers on top. Scoop out the flesh from the remaining passion or kiwi fruit and spoon it over the skewers. Sprinkle with a little toasted coconut, if you like, and garnish with slices of lime before serving.

Cool Green Fruit Salad

A sophisticated yet simple fruit salad for any time of year.

Serves 6

INGREDIENTS
3 Ogen or Galia melons
115 g/4 oz/1 cup green seedless grapes
1 kiwi fruit
1 star fruit
1 green-skinned apple
1 lime
175 ml/6 fl oz/¾ cup sparkling grape juice

1 Cut the melons in half and scoop out the seeds. Keeping the shells intact, scoop out the flesh with a melon baller, or scoop it out with a spoon and cut into bite-size cubes. Reserve the melon shells.

2 Remove any stems from the grapes. If the grapes are large, cut them in half. Peel and chop the kiwi fruit. Thinly slice the star fruit. Core and thinly slice the apple and place the slices in a bowl, together with the melon, grapes, kiwi fruit and star fruit.

3 Thinly pare the rind from the lime and cut it into fine strips. Blanch the strips for 30 seconds in boiling water, drain and rinse in cold water. Squeeze the juice from the lime and toss it into the fruit.

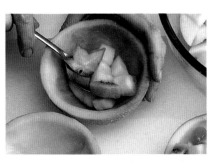

4 Spoon the prepared fruit into the reserved melon shells and chill in the fridge until required. Just before serving, spoon the sparkling grape juice over the fruit and scatter it with the lime rind.

COOK'S TIP: If you are serving this dessert on a hot summer day, arrange the melon shells on a platter of crushed ice. This will keep them beautifully cool.

Nutritional Notes	
Energy	91 Kcal/382 kJ
Fat, total	0.4 g
Saturated Fat	0.0 g
Cholesterol	0.0 mg

Mandarins in Syrup

Any lovely citrus fruits are suitable for this recipe.

Serves 4

INGREDIENTS
10 mandarins
15 ml/1 tbsp icing sugar
10 ml/2 tsp orange flower water
15 ml/1 tbsp chopped pistachio nuts

1 Thinly pare a little of the zest from one mandarin and cut it into fine shreds for decoration. Squeeze the juice from two of the mandarins and set aside.

2 Peel the remaining fruit, removing as much of the white pith as possible. Arrange the whole fruit in a wide dish.

3 Mix together the mandarin juice, icing sugar and orange flower water and pour it over the fruit. Cover the dish and chill in the fridge.

4 Blanch the shreds of mandarin zest in boiling water for 30 seconds. Drain, let cool and sprinkle them over the mandarins with the chopped pistachio nuts before serving.

Nutritional Notes	
Energy	91 Kcal/382 kJ
Fat, total	2.2 g
Saturated Fat	0.25 g
Cholesterol	0.0 mg

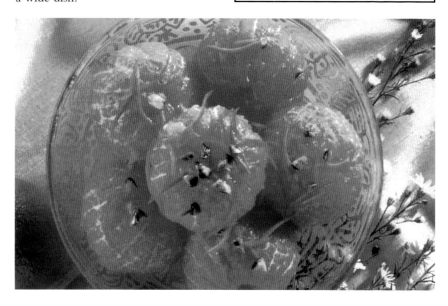

Figs with Ricotta Cream

Fresh, ripe figs are full of natural sweetness and need little adornment.

Serves 4

INGREDIENTS
4 ripe, fresh figs
115 g/4 oz/½ cup ricotta or cottage cheese
45 ml/3 tbsp low fat, thick natural yogurt or
  low fat crème fraîche
15 ml/1 tbsp clear honey
2.5 ml/½ tsp vanilla essence
freshly grated nutmeg, to decorate

1 Trim the stalks from the figs. Make four cuts through each fig from the stalk end, cutting them almost through, but leaving them joined at the base.

2 Place the figs on serving plates and open them out.

3 Mix together the ricotta or cottage cheese, yogurt or crème fraîche, honey and vanilla essence.

4 Spoon a little ricotta cream on to each plate and sprinkle with grated nutmeg to serve.

COOK'S TIP: The honey can be replaced with a little artificial sweetener.

Nutritional Notes	
Energy	97 Kcal/405 kJ
Fat, total	5.1 g
Saturated Fat	3.04 g
Cholesterol	26.2 mg

Pineapple Flambé

The flavour of alcohol burnt off by flambéing is not too overpowering.

Serves 4

INGREDIENTS
1 large, ripe pineapple
40 g/1½ oz/3 tbsp unsalted butter
45 ml/3 tbsp brown sugar
60 ml/4 tbsp fresh orange juice
30 ml/2 tbsp brandy
  or vodka
30 ml/2 tbsp slivered almonds,
  toasted
low fat crème fraîche or low fat,
  thick natural yogurt, to serve

1 Cut away the top and base of the pineapple. Then cut down the sides, removing all the dark 'eyes', but leaving the pineapple in good shape.

2 Cut the pineapple into thin slices and, with an apple corer, remove the hard central core. Prepare to fry the rings, preferably in one batch to avoid cooling.

3 Heat the butter, sugar and orange juice in a large frying pan. Add the pineapple slices and cook for about 1–2 minutes, turning once.

4 Add the brandy or vodka and carefully light with a long taper immediately. Let the flames die down and then sprinkle with the almonds. Serve with low fat crème fraîche or low fat, thick natural yogurt.

Nutritional Notes	
Energy	171 Kcal/711 kJ
Fat, total	5.0 g
Saturated Fat	0.62 g
Cholesterol	0.4 mg

VARIATION: You could substitute 4 thinly sliced apples for the pineapple.

RIGHT: *Pineapple Flambé and Warm Pears in Cider.*

Warm Pears in Cider

This dessert is simple to make, very attractive and tastes really delicious.

Serves 4

INGREDIENTS
1 lemon
50 g/2 oz/¼ cup caster sugar
a pinch of grated nutmeg
250 ml/8 fl oz/1 cup sweet cider
4 firm, ripe pears
freshly made skimmed-milk custard, low fat
    crème fraîche or low fat, thick natural
    yogurt, to serve

1 Carefully remove the rind from the lemon with a vegetable peeler, leaving any white pith behind. Squeeze the juice from the lemon into a saucepan, add the rind, sugar, nutmeg and cider and heat through to dissolve the sugar.

2 Carefully peel the pears, leaving the stalks intact, and place in the pan of cider. Poach, turning frequently with a spoon for 10–15 minutes, until almost tender.

3 With a slotted spoon, transfer the pears to individual serving dishes. Simmer the liquid over a high heat until it reduces slightly and becomes syrupy. Pour the warm syrup over the pears and serve as desired.

Nutritional Notes	
Energy	11 Kcal/46 kJ
Fat, total	0.0 g
Saturated Fat	0.0 g
Cholesterol	0.3 mg

Hot Bananas with Rum & Raisins

Use either all yellow or green-tipped bananas with no black patches.

Serves 4

INGREDIENTS
40 g/1½ oz/¼ cup seedless raisins
75 ml/5 tbsp dark rum
25 g/1 oz/2 tbsp unsalted butter
60 ml/4 tbsp soft, light brown sugar
1.5 ml/¼ teaspoon grated nutmeg
1.5 ml/¼ tsp ground cinnamon
4 ripe bananas, peeled and halved
    lengthways
30 ml/2 tbsp slivered almonds,
    toasted
chilled low fat crème fraîche or low fat, thick
    natural yogurt, to serve (optional)

1 Soak the raisins in the rum for 10 minutes. Dissolve the sugar in the melted butter and add the spices.

2 Add the bananas and cook until tender. Pour over the rum and raisins and set alight. Scatter with the almonds and serve.

Nutritional Notes	
Energy	263 Kcal/1110 kJ
Fat, total	4.1 g
Saturated Fat	0.5 g
Cholesterol	0.2 mg

Grilled Nectarines with Ricotta & Spice

Use canned peach halves in this easy dessert if fresh fruit is unavailable.

Serves 4

INGREDIENTS
4 ripe nectarines or peaches
15 ml/1 tbsp light muscovado sugar
115 g/4 oz/½ cup ricotta cheese or low fat
    crème fraîche
2.5 ml/½ tsp ground star anise

1 Preheat the grill to moderately hot. Cut the nectarines in half and remove the stones. Arrange the nectarines, cut side upwards, in a wide flameproof dish or on a non-stick baking sheet.

2 Stir the sugar into the ricotta or crème fraîche. Spoon the mixture into the hollow of each nectarine half.

3 Sprinkle with the star anise and grill for 6–8 minutes, or until the nectarines are hot and the filling is bubbling. Serve warm.

Nutritional Notes	
Energy	106 Kcal/450 kJ
Fat, total	3.3 g
Saturated Fat	2.0 g
Cholesterol	14.4 mg

Cornflake-topped Peach Bake

A golden, crisp-crusted family pudding that is made in minutes from storecupboard ingredients.

Serves 4

INGREDIENTS
415 g/14½ oz can peach slices in juice
30 ml/2 tbsp sultanas
1 cinnamon stick
strip of fresh orange rind
30 ml/2 tbsp butter or margarine
50 g/2 oz/1½ cups cornflakes
15 ml/1 tbsp sesame seeds

1 Preheat the oven to 200°C/400°F/ Gas 6. Drain the peaches, reserving the juice, and arrange the slices in a shallow ovenproof dish.

2 Place the juice, sultanas, cinnamon stick and orange rind in a pan and bring to the boil. Simmer, uncovered, for 3–4 minutes, until reduced by about half. Remove the cinnamon stick and orange rind.

3 Spoon the syrup over the drained peach slices and set aside while you prepare the topping.

4 Melt the butter or margarine in a small saucepan and stir in the cornflakes and sesame seeds. Mix well to coat thoroughly.

5 Spread the cornflake mixture over the fruit filling. Bake for 15–20 minutes, or until the topping is crisp and golden. Serve hot.

Nutritional Notes	
Energy	150 Kcal/633 kJ
Fat, total	4.6 g
Saturated Fat	1.0 g
Cholesterol	0.5 mg

Lychee & Elderflower Sorbet

The flavour of elderflowers complements lychees wonderfully.

Serves 4

INGREDIENTS
175 g/6 oz/1½ cup caster sugar
400 ml/14 fl oz/1⅔ cups water
500 g/1¼ lb fresh lychees, peeled
   and stoned
15 ml/1 tbsp elderflower cordial

1 Place the sugar and water in a saucepan and heat gently until the sugar has dissolved. Increase the heat and boil for 5 minutes, then add the lychees. Lower the heat and simmer for 7 minutes. Allow to cool.

2 Process the fruit and syrup in a blender or food processor. Press through a strainer with a spoon.

3 Stir the elderflower cordial into the strained purée, then pour the mixture into a freezerproof container. Freeze for 2 hours, until ice crystals start to form around the edges.

4 Remove from the freezer and process briefly in a blender or food processor. Repeat twice, then freeze until firm. Transfer the sorbet to the fridge for 10 minutes, to soften before serving.

Nutritional Notes	
Energy	249 Kcal/1058 kJ
Fat, total	0.1 g
Saturated Fat	0.0 g
Cholesterol	0.0 mg

Fresh Orange Granita

A granita is like a water ice with a grainier texture, hence its name.

Serves 6

INGREDIENTS
4 large oranges
1 large lemon
150 g/5 oz/⅔ cup sugar
475 ml/16 fl oz/2 cups water
blanched, pared strips of orange and
    lemon rind, to decorate

1 Thinly pare the rind from the oranges and lemon, taking care to avoid the bitter white pith, and set aside. Cut the fruit in half and squeeze the juice into a jug.

2 Heat the sugar and water in a heavy-based saucepan, stirring over a low heat until the sugar dissolves.

3 Bring to the boil, then boil without stirring for about 10 minutes, until a syrup forms.

4 Off the heat, add the rind and shake the pan. Cover until cool. Strain into a shallow freezerproof dish and add the reserved juice. Stir well, then freeze, uncovered, for about 4 hours, until slushy. Mix with a fork and return for 4 hours. Soften for 10 minutes before serving.

Nutritional Notes	
Energy	139 Kcal/589 kJ
Fat, total	0.2 g
Saturated Fat	0.0 g
Cholesterol	0.0 mg

Frozen Apple & Blackberry Terrine

Freeze this classic autumn combination to enjoy it at any time of year.

Serves 6

INGREDIENTS
500g/1¼ lb cooking or eating apples
300 ml/½ pint/1¼ cups sweet cider
15 ml/1 tbsp clear honey
5 ml/1 tsp vanilla essence
200 g/7 oz/1¼ cups fresh or frozen and
    thawed blackberries
15 ml/1 tbsp/1 envelope powdered gelatine
2 egg whites
fresh apple slices and blackberries, to
    decorate

1 Peel, core and chop the apples and place them in a pan with half the cider. Bring to the boil, cover and simmer until tender.

2 Purée the apples in a food processor. Stir in the honey and vanilla and remove half the purée. Add half the blackberries to the processor bowl and pulse until smooth. Press through a strainer to remove the pips.

3 Heat the remaining cider until it is almost boiling, then sprinkle the gelatine over it and stir until it has completely dissolved. Add half the cider to the apple purée and half to the blackberry and apple purée.

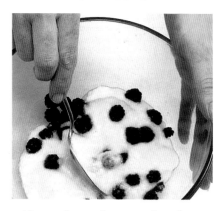

4 Leave the purées to cool until almost completely set. Whisk the egg whites until stiff. Quickly fold into the apple purée. Remove half the apple purée to another bowl. Stir the remaining whole blackberries into half the apple purée and then tip this into a 1.75 litre/3 pint/7½ cup loaf tin, packing down firmly.

5 Top with the blackberry and apple purée, spreading evenly. Add a layer of apple purée and smooth evenly. If necessary, freeze each layer until firm before adding the next.

6 Freeze until firm. To serve, allow to stand at room temperature for about 20 minutes to soften. Serve in slices with fresh apple slices and blackberries.

Nutritional Notes	
Energy	83 Kcal/346 kJ
Fat, total	0.2 g
Saturated Fat	0.0 g
Cholesterol	0.0 mg

Cappuccino Coffee Cups

Coffee-lovers will really enjoy this – and it tastes rich and creamy, even though it is very light.

Serves 4

INGREDIENTS
2 eggs
215 g/7½ oz carton evaporated
    semi-skimmed milk
25 ml/1½ tbsp instant coffee granules
    or powder
30 ml/2 tbsp sugar
10 ml/2 tsp powdered gelatine
60 ml/4 tbsp low fat,
    thick natural yogurt
cocoa powder or ground cinnamon,
    to decorate

1 Separate one egg and reserve the white. Beat the yolk with the whole of the remaining egg.

2 Put the evaporated milk, coffee granules or powder, sugar and beaten eggs in a pan and whisk until evenly combined.

3 Set the pan over a low heat and stir constantly until the mixture is hot, but not boiling, and is slightly thickened and smooth.

4 Remove the pan from the heat. Sprinkle the gelatine over the mixture and whisk until it has completely dissolved.

5 Spoon the coffee custard into four individual dishes or glasses and chill until well set.

6 Whisk the reserved egg white until it is stiff, adding the low fat yogurt, and then spoon the mixture over each individual glass or dish. Sprinkle the coffee cups with cocoa powder or ground cinnamon and serve.

COOK'S TIP: It is important to ensure that the gelatine is dissolved completely before spooning the mixture into the dishes, otherwise the texture will not be smooth.

Nutritional Notes	
Energy	146 Kcal/614 kJ
Fat, total	4.9 g
Saturated Fat	2.26 g
Cholesterol	115.1 mg

Fluffy Banana & Pineapple Mousse

This light, low fat mousse looks very impressive, but is really extremely easy to make, especially with a food processor.

Serves 6

INGREDIENTS
2 ripe bananas
225 g/8 oz/1 cup cottage cheese
425 g/15 oz can pineapple chunks or pieces in juice
15 ml/1 tbsp/1 envelope powdered gelatine
2 egg whites

1 Tie a double band of non-stick baking paper around a 600 ml/ 1 pint/2½ cup soufflé dish, to come 5 cm/2 in above the rim.

2 Peel and chop one banana and place it in a food processor with the cottage cheese. Process until smooth.

3 Drain the pineapple thoroughly, reserving the juice. Set aside a few chunks or pieces for decoration. Add the rest to the mixture in the food processor and process for a few seconds until finely chopped.

4 Dissolve the gelatine in 60 ml/ 4 tbsp of warmed pineapple juice. Stir the juice and gelatine quickly into the fruit mixture.

5 Whisk the egg whites until they form soft peaks and fold them lightly and evenly into the mixture. Tip the mousse mixture into the prepared dish, smooth the surface and chill in the fridge until set.

6 When the mousse is set, carefully remove the paper collar. Decorate the mousse with thin slices of the reserved banana and pineapple chunks.

Nutritional Notes	
Energy	108 Kcal/452 kJ
Fat, total	0.6 g
Saturated Fat	0.37 g
Cholesterol	1.9 mg

Lemon Hearts with Strawberry Sauce

These elegant hearts are as light as air. They are best made the day before.

Serves 6

INGREDIENTS

FOR THE HEARTS

175 g/6 oz/¾ cup ricotta cheese
150 ml/¼ pint/⅔ cup low fat crème fraîche
   or soured cream
15 ml/1 tbsp sugar
finely grated rind of ½ lemon
30 ml/2 tbsp lemon juice
10 ml/2 tsp powdered gelatine
2 egg whites

FOR THE SAUCE

225 g/8 oz/2 cups fresh or frozen
   and thawed strawberries
15 ml/1 tbsp lemon juice

1 Beat the ricotta cheese until smooth. Stir in the low fat crème fraîche, sugar and lemon rind with a wooden or metal spoon, until well mixed and thick.

2 Place the lemon juice in a small bowl and sprinkle the gelatine over it. Place the bowl over a pan of hot water and stir until the gelatine has completely dissolved.

3 Quickly stir the gelatine into the cheese mixture, mixing it in evenly.

4 Beat the egg whites until they form soft peaks. Quickly fold them into the cheese mixture.

5 Spoon the mixture into six lightly oiled, heart-shaped moulds and chill until set.

6 Reserve some strawberries for decoration. Place the remainder with the lemon juice in a blender or food processor and process until smooth. Pour on to serving plates and top with the turned-out hearts.

VARIATION: These little heart-shaped desserts are the perfect choice for a romantic dinner, but they needn't be heart-shaped: try setting the mixture in individual fluted moulds or even in teacups.

Nutritional Notes	
Energy	94 Kcal/397 kJ
Fat, total	4.2 g
Saturated Fat	2.60 g
Cholesterol	27.7 mg

Apricot & Pear Filo Roulade

This is a very quick way of making a strudel – normally very time consuming to do. It tastes delicious all the same!

Serves 4–6

INGREDIENTS
115 g/4 oz/½ cup ready-to-eat dried
   apricots, chopped
30 ml/2 tbsp apricot conserve
5 ml/1 tsp lemon juice
50 g/2 oz/4 tbsp light brown sugar
2 medium-size pears, peeled, cored and
   chopped
50 g/2 oz/½ cup ground almonds
30 ml/2 tbsp flaked almonds
8 sheets filo pastry,
   thawed if frozen
25 g/1 oz/2 tbsp butter, melted
icing sugar, to dust
low fat, thick natural yogurt or low fat
   crème fraîche, to serve

1 Put the apricots, apricot conserve, lemon juice, brown sugar and pears into a pan and heat gently, stirring continuously, for 5–7 minutes.

2 Remove from the heat and cool. Mix in the ground and flaked almonds. Preheat the oven to 200°C/400°F/Gas 6.

COOK'S TIP: This dessert can be frozen before cooking. Defrost the roulade completely on a baking tray.

3 Lightly grease a baking sheet. Layer the pastry on the baking sheet, brushing each layer with melted butter.

4 Spoon the filling down the pastry, just to one side of the centre, and within 2.5 cm/1 in of each end. Lift the other side of the pastry up by sliding a palette knife underneath.

5 Fold this pastry over the filling, tucking the edges under. Seal the ends neatly and brush all over with melted butter.

6 Bake the roulade for 15–20 minutes, until it is golden. Dust it with icing sugar and serve it hot, in individual portions, with low fat, thick natural yogurt or low fat crème fraîche.

Nutritional Notes	
Energy	190 Kcal/794 kJ
Fat, total	4.1 g
Saturated Fat	0.54 g
Cholesterol	0.1 mg

Filo Fruit Baskets

These colourful and light-as-air fruit baskets will just melt in your mouth.

Serves 6

INGREDIENTS

4 large or 8 small sheets of filo pastry,
   thawed if frozen
20 g/¾ oz/1½ tbsp butter or
   margarine, melted
250 ml/8 fl oz/1 cup low fat, thick
   natural yogurt
65 g/2½ oz/⅓ cup strawberry preserve
15 ml/1 tbsp Cointreau or other
   orange liqueur
115 g/4 oz/1 cup seedless red grapes,
   halved
115 g/4 oz/1 cup seedless green
   grapes, halved
115 g/4 oz/1 cup fresh pineapple cubes
175 g/6 oz/1 cup raspberries
30 ml/2 tbsp icing sugar
6 small sprigs of fresh mint,
   to decorate

1 Preheat the oven to 180°C/
350°F/Gas 4. Lightly grease a 6
cup, deep tartlet tin.

2 Stack the filo sheets and cut with a
sharp knife or scissors into 11 cm/
4½ in squares.

3 Lay four squares of pastry in each
of the tartlet tins. Press the pastry
firmly into the tins, rotating it slightly
to make star-shaped baskets.

4 Brush the pastry baskets lightly
with melted butter or margarine.
Bake for 5–7 minutes, until the pastry
is crisp and golden brown. Transfer to
a wire rack to cool.

5 In a bowl, lightly whip the
yogurt until soft peaks form.
Gently fold the strawberry preserve
and Cointreau into it.

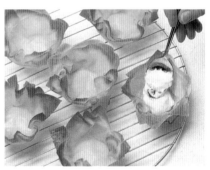

6 Just before serving, spoon a little
of the strawberry preserve mixture
into each pastry basket. Top with the
fruit. Sprinkle with the icing sugar
and decorate each basket with a
small sprig of mint.

Nutritional Notes	
Energy	235 Kcal/982 kJ
Fat, total	4.2 g
Saturated Fat	2.13 g
Cholesterol	9.3 mg

Apricot & Orange Roulade

This elegant dessert is very good served with a spoonful of low fat, thick natural yogurt or low fat crème fraîche.

Serves 6

INGREDIENTS
FOR THE ROULADE
4 egg whites
115 g/4 oz/½ cup golden
   caster sugar
50 g/2 oz/½ cup plain flour
finely grated rind of 1 small orange
45 ml/3 tbsp orange juice

FOR THE FILLING
115 g/4 oz/½ cup
   ready-to-eat dried apricots
150 ml/¼ pint/⅔ cup orange juice

TO DECORATE
10 ml/2 tsp icing sugar
shreds of orange zest

1 Preheat the oven to 200°C/400°F/ Gas 6. Grease a 23 x 33 cm/ 9 x 13 in Swiss roll tin and line it with non-stick baking paper. Grease the baking paper.

2 To make the roulade, place the egg whites in a large bowl and whisk until they form soft peaks. Gradually add the sugar, whisking hard between each addition. Fold in the flour, orange rind and juice. Spoon the mixture into the prepared tin and spread it evenly.

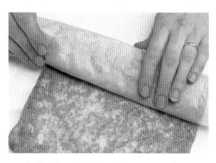

3 Bake for 15–18 minutes until golden. Turn out on to a sheet of non-stick baking paper and roll it up from one short side. Leave to cool.

4 Roughly chop the apricots and place them in a pan with the orange juice. Cover the pan and simmer until most of the liquid has been absorbed. Blend the apricots in a food processor to make a purée.

Nutritional Notes	
Energy	154 Kcal/652 kJ
Fat, total	0.3 g
Saturated Fat	0.01 g
Cholesterol	0.0 mg

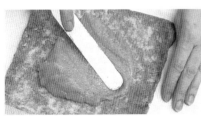

5 Unroll the roulade and spread with the apricot mixture. Roll up, arrange strips of paper diagonally across the roll, sprinkle lightly with lines of icing sugar, then remove the paper strips. Scatter the roulade with orange zest to serve.

Cinnamon Apple Gâteau

Make this lovely cake for an autumn celebration or dinner party dessert.

Serves 8

INGREDIENTS
3 eggs
115 g/4 oz/½ cup caster sugar
75 g/3 oz/⅔ cup plain flour
5 ml/1 tsp ground cinnamon

FOR THE FILLING AND TOPPING
4 large eating apples
60 ml/4 tbsp clear honey
15 ml/1 tbsp water
75 g/3 oz/½ cup sultanas
2.5 ml/½ tsp ground cinnamon
350 g/12 oz/1½ cups low fat soft cheese
60 ml/4 tbsp low fat fromage frais or ricotta
10 ml/2 tsp lemon juice
mint sprigs, to decorate

FOR THE APRICOT GLAZE
45 ml/3 tbsp apricot jam
dash of lemon juice

1 Preheat the oven to 190°C/375°F/ Gas 5. Grease and line a 23 cm/ 9 in sandwich cake tin. Place the eggs and sugar in a bowl and beat with a hand-held electric whisk until the mixture has the texture of mousse. When the whisk is lifted, a trail should remain on the surface of the mixture for at least 15 seconds.

2 Sift the flour and cinnamon over the egg mixture and carefully fold in with a large spoon.

3 Pour into the prepared tin and bake for 25–30 minutes or until the cake springs back when lightly pressed. Slide a palette knife around the cake to loosen the edge, then turn out on to a wire rack to cool.

4 To make the filling, peel, core and slice three of the apples and put them in a saucepan. Add 30 ml/2 tbsp of the honey and the water. Cover and cook over a low heat for about 10 minutes, or until the apples have softened. Add the sultanas and cinnamon, stir well, replace the lid and leave to cool.

5 Put the soft cheese in a bowl with the remaining honey, the fromage frais or ricotta and half the lemon juice. Beat until the mixture is smooth. Cut the cake in half horizontally, place the bottom half on a board and drizzle over any liquid from the apples. Spread with two thirds of the cheese mixture, then top with the apple filling. Fit the top of the cake in place.

6 To make the apricot glaze, heat the jam with the lemon juice over a low heat until it is runny. Press through a strainer and return to the pan to keep warm.

7 Swirl the remaining cheese mixture over the top of the cake. Slice the remaining apple, sprinkle with lemon juice and use to decorate the edge.

8 Brush the slices of apple with apricot glaze and place mint sprigs on top to decorate.

Nutritional Notes	
Energy	244 Kcal/1023 kJ
Fat, total	4.05 g
Saturated Fat	1.71 g
Cholesterol	77.95 mg

Tia Maria Gâteau

A feather-light coffee sponge with a creamy, liqueur-flavoured filling.

Serves 8

INGREDIENTS
75 g/3 oz/⅔ cup plain flour
30 ml/2 tbsp instant coffee powder
3 eggs
115 g/4 oz/½ cup caster sugar
coffee beans, to decorate (optional)

FOR THE FILLING
175 g/6 oz/¾ cup low fat soft cheese
15 ml/1 tbsp clear honey
15 ml/1 tbsp Tia Maria
50 g/2 oz/¼ cup stem ginger,
    roughly chopped

FOR THE MOCHA ICING
225 g/8 oz/2 cups icing sugar, sifted
10 ml/2 tsp coffee essence
15 ml/1 tbsp water
5 ml/1 tsp fat-reduced cocoa powder

1 Preheat the oven to 190°C/375°F/
Gas 5. Lightly grease and line a
deep, 20 cm/8 in round cake tin. Sift
together the plain flour and
coffee powder on to a sheet of
greaseproof paper.

2 In a bowl, whisk together the eggs
and sugar with a hand-held
electric whisk until thickened to the
texture of mousse. When the whisk
is lifted, a trail should remain on
the surface of the mixture for at
least 15 seconds.

3 Gently fold in the flour mixture
with a metal spoon. Turn the
mixture into the prepared tin. Bake
the sponge for 30–35 minutes, or until
it springs back when lightly pressed.
Turn out on to a wire rack to cool.

4 To make the filling, mix the soft
cheese with the honey in a bowl.
Beat until smooth, then add the Tia
Maria and stem ginger.

5 Cut the cake in half horizontally
and sandwich the two halves
together with the Tia Maria filling.

6 To make the mocha icing, mix the
icing sugar and coffee essence in a
bowl, with enough water to make an
icing which will coat the back of a
spoon. Pour three quarters over the
cake, spreading it evenly to the edges.
Stir the cocoa into the remaining icing
until smooth. Spoon into a piping bag
fitted with a writing nozzle.

7 Pipe the mocha icing over the coffee icing. Decorate with coffee beans, if liked.

Nutritional Notes	
Energy	226 Kcal/951 kJ
Fat, total	3.14 g
Saturated Fat	1.17 g
Cholesterol	75.03 mg

VARIATION: To make a mocha gâteau that is just as delicious, replace the coffee powder with 30 ml/2 tbsp fat-reduced cocoa powder, sifting it with the flour. Omit the chopped stem ginger from the filling. You might also like to experiment with other liqueurs for the gâteau filling such as Kahlua.

Blackberry Charlotte

A classic pudding, perfect for cold days. Serve with low fat, thick natural yogurt or skimmed-milk custard.

Serves 4

INGREDIENTS
40 g/1½ oz/3 tbsp unsalted butter
175 g/6 oz/3 cups fresh white breadcrumbs
50 g/2 oz/4 tbsp light brown sugar
60 ml/4 tbsp golden syrup
finely grated rind and juice of 2 lemons
50 g/2 oz/⅔ cup walnut halves
450 g/1 lb/4 cups blackberries
450 g/1 lb cooking apples, peeled, cored
and finely sliced

1 Preheat the oven to 180°C/350°F/ Gas 4. Grease a 450 ml/¾ pint/ 2 cup dish with 15 g/½ oz/1 tbsp of the butter. Melt the remaining butter. Add the breadcrumbs and sauté for 5–7 minutes, until crisp and golden. Leave to cool slightly.

2 Place the sugar, syrup, lemon rind and juice in a small saucepan and warm gently. Add the crumbs.

3 Process the walnuts until they are finely ground.

4 Arrange a thin layer of blackberries in the prepared dish. Top with a thin layer of crumbs. Add a thin layer of apple and cover it with another thin layer of crumbs.

5 Repeat with another layer of berries, followed by a layer of crumbs until you have used up all the ingredients, finishing with crumbs. The mixture should be piled well above the top edge of the dish because it shrinks during cooking. Bake for 30 minutes, until the crumbs are golden brown and the fruit is soft.

Nutritional Notes	
Energy	346 Kcal/1462 kJ
Fat, total	4.2 g
Saturated Fat	0.74 g
Cholesterol	0.5 mg

Sultana & Couscous Puddings

Most couscous on the market now is the pre-cooked variety, which needs only the minimum of cooking, but check the pack instructions first to make sure. Serve these puddings hot, with low fat, thick natural yogurt or skimmed-milk custard.

Serves 4

INGREDIENTS
50 g/2 oz/⅓ cup sultanas
475 ml/16 fl oz/2 cups
    apple juice
90 g/3½ oz/¾ cup couscous
2.5 ml/½ tsp mixed spice

1 Lightly grease four 250 ml/8 fl oz/ 1 cup pudding basins or one 1 litre/1¾ pint/4 cup pudding basin. Place the sultanas and apple juice in a small saucepan.

2 Bring the apple juice to the boil. Cover and simmer over a low heat for 2–3 minutes to plump up the fruit. Using a slotted spoon, lift out about half the fruit and place it in the bottom of the basins.

3 Add the couscous and mixed spice to the pan and bring back to the boil, stirring. Cover and cook over a low heat for 8–10 minutes, or until the liquid has been absorbed.

4 Spoon the couscous into the basins, spread it level and then cover the basins tightly with foil. Place the basins in a steamer over boiling water, cover and steam for about 30 minutes. Run a knife around the edges, carefully turn out the puddings and serve immediately.

Nutritional Notes	
Energy	132 Kcal/554 kJ
Fat, total	0.4 g
Saturated Fat	0.09 g
Cholesterol	0.0 mg

Chocolate, Date & Walnut Pudding

'Proper' puddings are not totally taboo when you are cutting down on fat or calories – this one stays within the rules. Serve hot with low fat, thick natural yogurt or skimmed-milk custard.

Serves 4

INGREDIENTS

15 g/½ oz/1 tbsp chopped walnuts
25 g/1 oz/2 tbsp chopped dates
1 egg, separated, plus 1 egg white
5 ml/1 tsp vanilla essence
30 ml/2 tbsp golden
    caster sugar
20 g/¾ oz/3 tbsp plain
    wholemeal flour
15 ml/1 tbsp cocoa powder
30 ml/2 tbsp skimmed milk

1 Preheat the oven to 180°C/350°F/ Gas 4. Grease a 1.2 litre/2 pint/ 5 cup pudding basin and place a small circle of greaseproof or non-stick baking paper in the base. Spoon in the walnuts and dates.

2 Place the egg yolk in a bowl with the vanilla and sugar. Place the bowl over a pan of hot water and whisk until the mixture is thick and pale. Remove the bowl from the heat.

3 Sift the flour and cocoa into the mixture and fold them in with a metal spoon. Stir in the milk to soften the mixture slightly. Whisk the egg whites until they form soft peaks and fold them in.

Nutritional Notes	
Energy	126 Kcal/530 kJ
Fat, total	4.9 g
Saturated Fat	1.15 g
Cholesterol	48.3 mg

4 Spoon the mixture into the pudding basin and bake for 40–45 minutes, or until the pudding is well risen and firm to the touch. Run a knife around the pudding to loosen it from the basin and then turn it out. Serve immediately.

47

Fruit & Spice Bread Pudding

An easy-to-make fruity dessert with a hint of spice, which is delicious served either hot or cold.

Serves 4

INGREDIENTS
6 medium slices wholemeal bread
50 g/2 oz/⅓ cup jam
50 g/2 oz/⅓ cup sultanas
50 g/2 oz/¼ cup ready-to-eat dried
   apricots, chopped
50 g/2 oz/4 tbsp light brown sugar
5 ml/1 tsp ground mixed spice
2 eggs
600 ml/1 pint/2½ cups skimmed milk
finely grated rind of 1 lemon

2 Mix together the sultanas, apricots, sugar and spice and sprinkle half the fruit mixture over the bread in the ovenproof dish.

3 Top with the remaining bread and jam triangles and then sprinkle them with the remaining fruit mixture.

1 Preheat the oven to 160°C/325°F/ Gas 3. Remove the crusts from the bread, spread with jam and cut into small triangles. Place half the triangles in a lightly greased ovenproof dish.

4 Beat the eggs, milk and lemon rind together and pour the mixture over the bread. Set aside for about 30 minutes to allow the bread to absorb some of the liquid. Bake for 45–60 minutes, until lightly set and golden brown. Serve hot or cold.

Nutritional Notes	
Energy	305 Kcal/1293 kJ
Fat, total	4.51 g
Saturated Fat	1.27 g
Cholesterol	0.0 mg

Hot Blackberry & Apple Soufflés

As the blackberry season is so short and the apple season is so long, it is worth freezing a bag of blackberries to have on hand for treats like this.

Serves 4

INGREDIENTS

low fat spread, for greasing
150 g/5 oz/⅔ cups caster sugar, plus extra
    for dusting
350 g/12 oz/2 cups blackberries
1 large cooking apple, peeled, cored and
    finely diced
grated rind and juice of 1 orange
3 egg whites
icing sugar, for dusting

1 Preheat the oven to 200°C/400°F/ Gas 6. Generously grease four 150 ml/¼ pint/⅔ cup individual soufflé dishes with low fat spread and dust with caster sugar, shaking out the excess sugar. Put a baking sheet in the oven to heat.

2 Cook the blackberries and diced apple with the orange rind and juice in a pan for 10 minutes, or until the apple has pulped down well. Press through a strainer, using a wooden spoon or ladle, into a bowl. Stir in 50 g/2 oz/¼ cup of the caster sugar. Set aside to cool.

3 Put a spoonful of the fruit purée into each prepared dish and smooth the surface. Set the dishes aside.

4 Whisk the egg whites until they form stiff peaks. Very gradually whisk in the remaining caster sugar to make a stiff, glossy meringue mixture.

5 Fold in the remaining fruit purée and spoon the flavoured meringue into each prepared dish. Level the tops with a palette knife and run a table knife around the edge of each dish. Place the dishes on the hot baking sheet and bake for 10–15 minutes, until the soufflés have risen well and are lightly browned. Dust the tops with icing sugar and serve immediately.

Nutritional Notes	
Energy	138 Kcal/584 kJ
Fat, total	0.3 g
Saturated Fat	0.5 g
Cholesterol	0.0 mg

Summer Pudding

Do not reserve this lovely pudding solely for summer. It freezes well and provides a delicious dessert for Christmas Day, as a light and refreshing alternative to the traditional pudding.

Serves 4–6

INGREDIENTS

8 x 1 cm/½ in thick slices of day-old white
    bread, crusts removed
800 g/1¾ lb/6–7 cups mixed berry fruits,
    such as strawberries, raspberries,
    blackcurrants, redcurrants and blueberries
50 g/2 oz/¼ cup golden caster sugar
low fat, thick natural yogurt or low fat crème
    fraîche, to serve

1 Trim a slice of the bread to fit in the base of a 1 litre/1¾ pint/4 cups pudding basin, then trim another 5–6 slices to line the sides of the basin.

2 Place all the fruit in a heavy-based saucepan with the sugar. Cook gently, uncovered, for 4–5 minutes, until the juices begin to run – it will not be necessary to add any water. Allow the mixture to cool slightly.

3 Spoon the berries, and juice to moisten, into the bread-lined basin. Save any leftover juice for serving.

4 Fold over the excess bread, then cover the fruit with the remaining bread slices, trimming to fit. Place a small plate directly on top of the pudding, fitting it inside the basin. Weight it with a 900 g/2 lb weight, if you have one, or use full cans.

5 Chill in the fridge for at least 8 hours or overnight. To serve, run a knife around the pudding and turn on to a plate. Serve with juice and yogurt or crème fraîche.

Nutritional Notes	
Energy	266 Kcal/1131 kJ
Fat, total	1.7 g
Saturated Fat	0.28 g
Cholesterol	0.0 mg

Soft Fruit Pavlova

This is the queen of desserts and is ideal for a special occasion.

Serves 4

INGREDIENTS
4 egg whites
175 g/6 oz/¾ cup caster sugar
30 ml/2 tbsp redcurrant jelly
15 ml/1 tbsp rose water
300 ml/½ pint/1¼ cups low fat,
    thick natural yogurt or
    low fat crème fraîche
450 g/1 lb/4½ cups mixed soft fruits,
    such as blackberries, blueberries
    redcurrants, raspberries or
    loganberries
10 ml/2 tsp icing sugar, sifted
pinch of salt

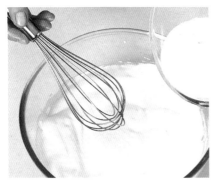

1 Preheat the oven to 140°C/275°F/
Gas 1. Lightly oil a baking sheet.
Whisk the egg whites with a pinch of
salt in a grease-free bowl until they are
white and standing in firm peaks.
Gradually whisk in the caster sugar
and continue to whisk until the
mixture is stiff and glossy.

2 Spoon the meringue into a 25 cm/
10 in round on the baking sheet,
making a slight indentation in the
centre and soft crests around the edge.

3 Bake for 1–1½ hours until the
meringue is firm. Check it
frequently, as the meringue can easily
overcook and turn brown. Transfer the
meringue to a serving plate.

4 Melt the redcurrant jelly in a small
bowl set over a pan of hot water.
Cool slightly, then spread the jelly in
the centre of the meringue.

5 Mix the rose water with the yogurt
or crème fraîche and spoon into
the centre of the meringue. Place the
fruits on top and dust with icing sugar.

Nutritional Notes	
Energy	302 Kcal/1280 kJ
Fat, total	3.9 g
Saturated Fat	2.37 g
Cholesterol	5.3 mg

Tofu Berry 'Cheesecake'

This summery 'cheesecake' is a very light and refreshing finish to any meal. Strictly speaking it is not a cheesecake at all, as it is based on tofu – but who would guess?

Serves 6

INGREDIENTS

FOR THE BASE
50 g/2 oz/4 tbsp low fat spread
30 ml/2 tbsp apple juice
115 g/4 oz/2½ cups bran flakes or other high fibre cereal

FOR THE FILLING
275 g/10 oz/1¼ cups tofu or skimmed-milk soft cheese
200 ml/7 fl oz/⅞ cup low fat, thick natural yogurt
15 ml/1 tbsp/1 envelope powdered gelatine
60 ml/4 tbsp apple juice

FOR THE TOPPING
175 g/6 oz/1¾ cups mixed soft fruit, such as strawberries, raspberries, redcurrants and blackberries, or frozen 'fruits of the forest', thawed
30 ml/2 tbsp redcurrant jelly
30 ml/2 tbsp hot water

1 To make the base, place the low fat spread and apple juice in a pan over a low heat. Crush the cereal and stir it into the pan. Tip into a 23 cm/ 9 in round flan tin and press down firmly. Chill the base in the fridge until set.

2 To make the filling, place the tofu or cheese and yogurt in a food processor and process until smooth. Sprinkle the gelatine in the apple juice to soften, blend until it has completely dissolved, then quickly stir it into the tofu or cheese mixture.

3 Spread the tofu or cheese mixture over the cake base, smoothing it evenly. Chill in the fridge until the filling is set.

4 Remove the flan tin and place the 'cheesecake' on a serving plate. Arrange the fruits over the top. Melt the redcurrant jelly with the hot water. Let it cool, then spoon it over the fruit to serve.

Nutritional Notes	
Energy	163 Kcal/688 kJ
Fat, total	4.4 g
Saturated Fat	0.93 g
Cholesterol	1.6 mg

Raspberry Vacherin

Meringue rounds with an orange-flavoured filling combined with fresh raspberries make a perfect dinner party dessert.

Serves 6

INGREDIENTS
3 egg whites
175 g/6 oz/¾ cup caster sugar
5 ml/1 tsp chopped almonds
icing sugar, for dusting
raspberry leaves, to decorate

FOR THE FILLING
175 g/6 oz/¾ cup low fat soft cheese
15–30 ml/1–2 tbsp clear honey
15 ml/1 tbsp Cointreau or other
    orange-flavoured liqueur
120 ml/4 fl oz/½ cup low fat, thick natural
    yogurt or low fat crème fraîche
225 g/8 oz/1⅓ cups raspberries

1 Preheat the oven to 140°C/275°F/ Gas 1. Draw a 20 cm/8 in circle on two pieces of non-stick baking paper. Turn the paper over so the marking is on the underside and use it to line two heavy baking sheets.

2 Whisk the egg whites in a grease-free bowl until very stiff. Gradually whisk in the caster sugar until the mixture is stiff and glossy.

COOK'S TIP: Whisk the egg whites until they are so stiff that you can turn the bowl upside down without them falling out.

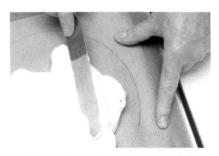

3 Spoon the mixture into the circles on the baking sheets, spreading the meringue evenly to the edges. Sprinkle one meringue round with the chopped almonds.

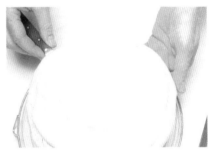

4 Bake for 1½–2 hours, then carefully lift the meringue rounds off the baking sheets, peel away the paper and cool on wire racks.

5 To make the filling, cream the soft cheese with the honey and liqueur in a bowl. Fold in the yogurt or low fat crème fraîche and most of the raspberries, reserving the three best ones for decoration.

6 Place the plain meringue on a board, spread with the filling and top with the nut-covered round. Dust with icing sugar, transfer to a plate and decorate with the reserved raspberries and a sprig of raspberry leaves.

Nutritional Notes	
Energy	244 Kcal/1023 kJ
Fat, total	4.05 g
Saturated Fat	1.71 g
Cholesterol	77.95 mg

Banana, Maple & Lime Pancakes

Pancakes are always a treat and can be made in advance and frozen. They take only a few minutes to defrost.

Serves 4

INGREDIENTS
115 g/4 oz/1 cup plain flour
1 egg white
250 ml/8 fl oz/1 cup skimmed milk
50 ml/2 fl oz/¼ cup water
sunflower oil, for frying

FOR THE FILLING
4 bananas, sliced
45 ml/3 tbsp maple syrup or golden syrup
30 ml/2 tbsp lime juice
strips of lime rind, to decorate

1 Beat together the flour, egg white, milk and water until smooth and bubbly. Chill until required.

2 Heat a little oil in a non-stick frying pan, pour in enough batter to coat the base, cook until golden, loosen with a spatula, and toss. Remove from pan and keep hot.

3 For the filling, simmer the bananas, syrup and lime juice in a pan for one minute. Spoon into the pancakes and fold into quarters. Decorate with lime rind and serve hot.

Nutritional Notes	
Energy	282 Kcal/1185 kJ
Fat, total	2.79 g
Saturated Fat	0.47 g
Cholesterol	1.25 mg

Lemon & Lime Sauce

A tangy, refreshing sauce, which is delicious with Banana, Maple & Lime

Pancakes or fruit tarts.

Serves 4

INGREDIENTS
1 lemon
2 limes
50 g/2 oz/¼ cup caster sugar
25 ml/1½ tbsp arrowroot
300 ml/½ pint/1¼ cups water
lemon balm or mint,
    to garnish

1 Using a citrus zester, thinly pare the lemon and lime rinds. Squeeze the juice from the fruit.

2 Place the rind in a pan, cover with water and bring to the boil. Drain and set the rind aside.

3 In a small bowl, mix a little sugar with the arrowroot. Blend in enough water to make a smooth paste. Heat the remaining water in a small pan, pour in the arrowroot mixture and stir constantly until the sauce boils and thickens.

4 Stir in the remaining sugar, citrus juice and rinds. Decorate with the lemon balm or mint and serve hot.

Nutritional Notes	
Energy	75 Kcal/317 kJ
Fat, total	0.1 g
Saturated Fat	0.0 g
Cholesterol	0.0 mg

Floating Islands in Hot Plum Sauce

An unusual pudding that is simpler to make than it looks. The sauce can be made in advance and reheated just before you cook the meringues.

Serves 4

INGREDIENTS
450 g/1 lb red plums
300 ml/½ pint/1¼ cups apple juice
2 egg whites
30 ml/2 tbsp concentrated apple juice syrup
freshly grated nutmeg

1 Cut the plums in half and remove the stones. Place them in a wide pan with the apple juice.

2 Bring to the boil, cover and simmer gently over a low heat until the plums are tender, but still retain their shape. Test with the tip of a sharp knife for softness.

3 While the plums are cooking, whisk the egg whites in a grease-free metal or glass bowl until soft peaks form.

4 Gradually whisk in the apple juice syrup and continue whisking until the meringue forms quite firm peaks.

5 Using a tablespoon, scoop the meringue into the simmering plum sauce in two batches.

6 Cover and simmer for about 2–3 minutes, until the meringues are just set. Serve immediately, sprinkled with a little freshly grated nutmeg.

COOK'S TIP: If you cannot obtain apple juice syrup, use clear honey.

Nutritional Notes	
Energy	77 Kcal/324 kJ
Fat, total	0.3 g
Saturated Fat	0.0 g
Cholesterol	0.0 mg

Index

This edition published by Hermes House

Hermes House is an imprint of
Anness Publishing Limited
Hermes House, 88–89 Blackfriars Road, London SE1 8HA

Publisher: Joanna Lorenz
Editor: Valerie Ferguson
Series Designer: Bobbie Colgate Stone
Designer: Andrew Heath
Editorial Reader: Kate Henderson
Production Controller: Joanna King

Recipes contributed by: Angela Boggiano,
Frances Cleary, Nicola Diggins, Christine France,
Shirley Gill, Carole Handslip, Gilly Love,
Maggie Mayhew, Anne Sheasby, Liz Trigg, Jeni Wright.

Photography: William Adams-Lingwood, Karl Adamson,
Steve Baxter, James Duncan, Michelle Garrett,
Amanda Heywood, David Jordan, Don Last,
Thomas Odulate.

© Anness Publishing Limited 1999, updated 2000

2 3 4 5 6 7 8 9 10

Notes:
For all recipes, quantities are given in both metric and
imperial measures and, where appropriate, measures are
also given in standard cups and spoons.
Follow one set, but not a mixture, because they are
not interchangeable.
Standard spoon and cup measures are level.
1 tsp = 5 ml
1 tbsp = 15 ml
1 cup = 250 ml/8 fl oz

Australian standard tablespoons are 20 ml.
Australian readers should use 3 tsp in place of 1 tbsp for
measuring small quantities of gelatine, cornflour, salt, etc.

Medium eggs are used unless otherwise stated.

Publisher's Note: Nutritional Notes are based on fat per
serving and do not include optional decorations.

Printed and bound in China